Life Story of Saint Eusebius of Vercelli, Bishop

Defender of Faith, Champion of Orthodoxy

Cathleen F. Hogan

Table of Contents

Introduction

In the fourth century, a man by the name of Eusebius resided in the modern Italian city of Vercelli. He had no idea that he would go on to become a beloved saint and a powerful bishop in the early Christian Church.

Eusebius was raised by godly parents and had a good education. His parents instilled in him a strong sense of faith and a love for the Church. As he grew older, Eusebius had a deep desire to devote his life to helping God and His people.

Eusebius experienced a great spiritual conversion as a result of the Christian teachings. He fully embraced the faith and pledged himself to God's service. Observing his fervor and dedication, the Church ordained him as a priest.

Eusebius' reputation as a holy and knowledgeable priest spread far and wide. He became known for his defense of orthodox Christian doctrine and his opposition to the heretical teachings of Arianism, which denied the divinity of Jesus Christ. Eusebius firmly believed in the divinity of Christ and tirelessly preached and debated to uphold this fundamental truth.

His unwavering commitment to orthodoxy caught the attention of the Church hierarchy, and Eusebius was appointed as the Bishop of Vercelli. With this new position of authority, he faced numerous challenges. Arianism had gained significant influence, and many clergy and followers embraced its teachings. However, Eusebius fearlessly stood against the heresy, knowing that it was crucial for the Church to uphold the true nature of Christ.

Eusebius actively participated in the Council of Alexandria, where he defended the orthodox faith and contributed to the formulation of Church doctrine. His eloquence and unwavering conviction played a significant role in the council's decisions, as he helped strengthen the Church's understanding of the Trinity.

However, Eusebius' stance against Arianism did not go unnoticed or unopposed. The Arian authorities, threatened by his influence, sought to silence him. Eusebius was exiled from his beloved city of Vercelli and sent to Scythopolis, a distant region far from his flock.

Despite the hardships of exile, Eusebius continued to lead and inspire. He established monastic communities in Scythopolis, providing spiritual guidance and fostering a strong sense of community among the faithful. His influence transcended physical boundaries, as he maintained correspondence with other prominent

Church leaders, such as Saint Athanasius and Saint Basil the Great.

Years later, due to the changing political landscape and the persistence of his supporters, Eusebius was allowed to return from exile. He spent his final years back in Vercelli, dedicated to his pastoral duties and guiding his flock. His teachings and writings on theology and liturgy greatly impacted the Church, and his monastic foundations continued to thrive.

Saint Eusebius of Vercelli passed away, leaving behind a lasting legacy. He was venerated as a saint for his unwavering faith, his defense of orthodox doctrine, and his profound influence on the early

Christian Church. The Church officially recognized his sanctity, and his feast day was established to honor his memory.

Even today, Saint Eusebius of Vercelli is remembered as a shining example of steadfast faith, unwavering dedication, and courageous defense of Christian truth. His life serves as an inspiration for all believers, reminding them to remain firm in their convictions and to never waver in their commitment to God and His Church.

Overview of Saint Eusebius of Vercelli

Early Christian bishop and saint Eusebius of Vercelli, also known as Eusebius of Vercelli, lived in the fourth century. In or around the year 283, he was born in Sardinia, Italy. Eusebius was raised in a strict religious environment and hailed from a family of devoted Christians. He committed his entire life to serving God and rose to fame for his steadfast adherence to traditional Christian teaching.

Eusebius achieved success as a priest and acquired a reputation for standing up for the righteous religion against the false teachings of Arianism. Arianism denied that Jesus Christ was divine; Eusebius vehemently battled this error and steadfastly upheld the doctrine of Christ's deity.

The Church authority took note of his expertise and constancy, and he was chosen to serve as the bishop of Vercelli in present-day Italy. As a bishop, Eusebius faced numerous challenges, particularly in combating the spread of Arianism among clergy and followers.

Eusebius played a significant role in the Council of Alexandria, where he defended the orthodox faith and contributed to the formulation of Church doctrine. His teachings and arguments greatly influenced the council's decisions, strengthening the Church's understanding of the Trinity.

However, his opposition to Arianism led to his exile. Eusebius was banished from Vercelli and spent several years in Scythopolis, a distant region. Despite the hardships of exile, he continued to lead and inspire, establishing monastic communities and maintaining correspondence with other prominent Church leaders.

After his return from exile, Eusebius dedicated himself to his pastoral duties and the spiritual guidance of his flock in Vercelli. His teachings on theology and liturgy had a profound impact on the Church, and his monastic foundations flourished.

Saint Eusebius of Vercelli is revered as a saint for his unwavering faith, defense of orthodox doctrine, and his contributions to the early Christian Church. His life serves as an example of steadfast commitment to the truth and courageous leadership. Today, he is remembered and venerated for his significant influence on the development of Christian theology and his enduring legacy as a holy bishop.

Importance and significance of his life and ministry

Saint Eusebius of Vercelli's life and work have had a significant impact on the development of the Christian Church. Here are a few main justifications

Orthodoxy is defended

In order to combat the growth of Arianism, Eusebius was instrumental in upholding traditional Christian theology. His uncompromising adherence to the doctrine of Jesus Christ's deity—as opposed to Arianism, which denied Christ's deity—helped keep the fundamental principles of the religion alive. The establishment of accurate theological understanding throughout the Church was made possible by Eusebius' unwavering adherence to orthodoxy.

Alexandrian Council

A notable assembly of bishops held in Alexandria to address the Arian problem included Eusebius among its participants. His input into the council's discussions helped mold the Church's conception of the Trinity and reaffirmed the divinity of Jesus Christ. Eusebius's theological insights and persuasive arguments played a vital role in upholding orthodox Christian teachings.

Exile and Persecution

Eusebius's exile from Vercelli due to his opposition to Arianism highlights the challenges he faced in defending the faith. His exile demonstrates the extent to which he was willing to endure personal hardships and separation from his community to safeguard the truth. Eusebius's steadfastness in the face of persecution serves as a powerful example of courage and conviction for believers throughout history.

Monastic Foundations

Eusebius established monastic communities during his exile, which became centers of spiritual growth, prayer, and Christian living. These communities not only provided support and refuge for believers during turbulent times but also contributed to the spread of monasticism and its positive influence on the Church. Eusebius's dedication to fostering monastic life left a lasting impact on the spiritual development of individuals and the broader Christian community.

Correspondence and Relationships

Eusebius maintained correspondence with other influential Church leaders of his time, such as Saint Athanasius and Saint Basil the Great. His interactions and exchanges of ideas helped foster unity within the Church and contributed to the development of theological thought. Eusebius's relationships with these prominent figures highlight his standing as a respected and trusted leader in the Church.

Veneration and Legacy

Saint Eusebius of Vercelli is venerated as a saint for his holiness, unwavering faith, and contributions to the Church. His life and ministry continue to inspire believers, serving as a reminder of the importance of defending the truth and upholding orthodox Christian doctrine. Eusebius's influence on the development of Christian theology, his courageous leadership, and his enduring legacy as a holy bishop make him a significant figure in the history of the Church.

Overall, Saint Eusebius of Vercelli's life and ministry were characterized by his defense of orthodoxy, his role in the Council of Alexandria, his endurance through exile and persecution, his establishment of monastic communities, and his relationships with other Church leaders. His contributions and the significance of his example continue to resonate with believers, emphasizing the importance of upholding and preserving the true teachings of the Christian faith.

Chapter 2: Early Life and Education

Around the year 283, in Sardinia, Italy, the saint Eusebius of Vercelli was born. He was raised in a devoted Christian home where he received a strong foundation in faith and a love for the Church. Eusebius had a good education, which gave him the knowledge and sharp mind that would later help him to shape his ministry.

Eusebius probably learned about the Bible and Christian doctrines via his family and the nearby Christian community when he was a young child. His foundation for his spiritual journey and eventual commitment to God's service was built by this early introduction to the faith.

Beyond religious instruction, Eusebius received a broad education. Since literature, philosophy, and rhetoric were prized disciplines in classical education, it is possible that he had a more extensive education that included all three of these subjects of the time. This well-rounded education would later contribute to his eloquence and ability to effectively communicate and defend the orthodox Christian faith.

Eusebius's education and upbringing played a crucial role in preparing him for his future ministry. The knowledge and understanding he gained through his education, combined with his strong faith and devotion, shaped him into a formidable defender of orthodox doctrine and a leader within the Church.

It is worth noting that specific details about Saint Eusebius's early life and education are limited. Historical records primarily focus on his ministry and contributions to the Church, with less information available about his formative years. However, his subsequent achievements and impact on the early Christian Church indicate that his early life and education laid a solid foundation for his remarkable journey as a bishop and saint.

Birth and family background

In Sardinia, Italy, about the year 283, Saint Eusebius of Vercelli was born. Even if there isn't a lot of information available about his family history, his birthplace indicates that he is of Sardinian descent.

Since Eusebius was raised in a devoted Christian household, it is possible that his parents played a key role in forming his religious beliefs. His spiritual path and eventual consecration to the service of God were made possible by their influence and teachings.

His parents' names and occupations are unfortunately unknown due to incomplete historical records. However, it is clear that their adherence to Christianity and the morals they imparted in Eusebius played a significant role in forming his personality, religion, and ultimate calling as a bishop.

Eusebius adopted a life of religious service, which indicates that his family had a strong Christian identity and may have been involved in the Christian community of their time. This familial support and religious upbringing likely played a significant role in shaping his early beliefs and nurturing his spiritual growth.

While the details of Saint Eusebius's birth and family background are not extensively documented, his subsequent life and accomplishments illustrate the profound impact of his upbringing and the influence of his Christian heritage. His dedication to the Church and defense of orthodox Christian doctrine stand as a testament to the formative influence of his family's faith and the values they imparted to him.

Education and early influences

Through a quality education, Saint Eusebius of Vercelli acquired the knowledge and skills that were essential to his subsequent ministry. Despite the lack of particular information on his schooling, it can be assumed that he obtained a thorough and well-rounded education for the time.

From a young age, Eusebius most certainly got instruction in the Bible and Christian doctrine from both his family and the nearby Christian community. His spiritual growth and eventual devotion to serving God would have been laid out by this early exposure to the faith.

Eusebius would have acquired a broader education that included coursework in disciplines like literature, philosophy, and rhetoric in addition to his religious education. In the time's classical education, these subjects were prized, and played a significant role in shaping one's intellectual abilities and communication skills.

Eusebius's education in literature would have exposed him to the works of both pagan and Christian writers. This familiarity with different literary traditions and styles likely influenced his own writing and helped him effectively convey his ideas and defend orthodox Christian teachings.

The study of philosophy would have provided Eusebius with critical thinking skills and a deeper understanding of metaphysical and ethical concepts. This knowledge would have been valuable in engaging with philosophical ideas and responding to challenges against Christian doctrine.

Rhetoric, the art of persuasive communication, was another important aspect of Eusebius's education. Mastery of rhetoric allowed him to deliver compelling speeches, engage in debates, and effectively convey his beliefs to others. His eloquence and persuasive abilities were renowned and played a significant role in his defense of orthodox Christianity.

Eusebius's education and early influences, which combined religious instruction, exposure to various literary traditions, philosophical studies, and rhetorical training, equipped him with the intellectual tools necessary for his later ministry. These formative years provided him with a solid foundation of knowledge, reasoning skills, and effective communication, enabling him to become a prominent defender of the Christian faith and an influential bishop in the early Church.

Chapter 3. Conversion and Ordination

The great spiritual transformation that caused Saint Eusebius of Vercelli to accept Christianity and devote his life to serving God was the result of his tremendous spiritual awakening. Although there isn't a lot of information available on the specifics of his conversion, it is known that he underwent a profound change in his beliefs and wholeheartedly embraced Christianity.

The religious upbringing in his family, the teachings of the early Christian communities, as well as Eusebius's own experiences and observations, all likely had an impact on his conversion. His early convictions and the development of a solid foundation of religion would have been significantly shaped by the impact of his family's fervent Christian upbringing, in particular.

Eusebius felt a desire to serve God and His people when he was converted, and he began by a more dedicated manner. This led him to pursue ordination as a priest, a step that marked his formal entry into the clergy and set him on the path of ministering to the faithful.

Ordination as a priest involved a liturgical ceremony and the laying on of hands by a bishop or other ordained priests. Through this sacramental act, Eusebius was set apart for sacred service and bestowed with the authority to celebrate the Eucharist, administer the sacraments, and provide pastoral care to the Christian community.

As a priest, Eusebius would have been actively involved in the life of the Church, offering spiritual guidance, preaching, and participating in the liturgy. His dedication, knowledge, and passion for the faith likely gained him a reputation as a holy and knowledgeable priest, paving the way for his subsequent appointment as the Bishop of Vercelli.

The conversion and ordination of Saint Eusebius of Vercelli mark significant milestones in his spiritual journey and commitment to the Christian faith. His conversion reflects a personal encounter with the teachings and message of Christ, while his ordination as a priest signifies his willingness to serve God and His Church in a leadership capacity. These pivotal moments laid the groundwork for his influential ministry and his subsequent defense of orthodox Christian doctrine.

Spiritual journey and conversion to Christianity

Few specifics about Saint Eusebius of Vercelli's spiritual development and conversion to Christianity have been recorded. Though it is known that he suffered a significant transition that prompted him to accept Christianity and commit his life to serving God, it is unknown how this transformation occurred.

It is possible that Eusebius personally encountered the ideas and message of Christ on his spiritual journey. The religious climate in his family, the influence of Christian communities in his area, as well as his own experiences and views may have all had an impact.

Eusebius would have been steeped in the doctrines of the faith from an early age having grown up in a devoted Christian home. His family instilled in him strong Christian ideals, and he often attended Christian gatherings and worship services that would have laid a foundation for his spiritual development.

As he matured, Eusebius may have encountered the teachings of Christian leaders and witnessed the transformative power of the Gospel in the lives of believers. This exposure to the Christian community and the witness of others' faith may have sparked a curiosity and deep longing within him to understand and experience the truth of Christianity for himself.

Eusebius's personal experiences, reflections, and inner seeking likely played a significant role in his spiritual journey. It is through this journey that he came to recognize the truth and significance of the Christian faith, leading to a profound conversion experience.

The exact circumstances and details of Eusebius's conversion are not recorded, but his decision to fully embrace Christianity would have involved a conscious choice and a surrender of his life to Christ. This conversion marked a turning point in his life, as he committed himself wholeheartedly to the teachings and values of the Christian faith.

Eusebius's conversion set him on a path of dedicated service to God and His people. His newfound faith and commitment to Christ fueled his passion for the Church and led him to pursue a life of ministry, eventually becoming a bishop and a prominent defender of orthodox Christian doctrine.

While the specifics of Saint Eusebius's spiritual journey and conversion remain largely unknown, his profound dedication to the Christian faith and his subsequent contributions to the Church serve as a testament to the transformative power of encountering Christ and embracing His teachings.

Ordination as a priest

After Saint Eusebius of Vercelli underwent his spiritual conversion and dedicated his life to the Christian faith, he pursued ordination as a priest. Ordination marked his formal entry into the clergy and equipped him with the authority to carry out sacred duties and provide spiritual guidance to the faithful.

The process of ordination as a priest in the early Christian Church involved a liturgical ceremony and the laying on of hands by a bishop or other ordained priests. This act symbolized the impartation of the Holy Spirit and the conferral of spiritual authority upon the candidate.

Through his ordination, Eusebius was set apart for sacred service and granted the authority to perform various priestly functions. These responsibilities included celebrating the Eucharist, administering the sacraments, preaching and teaching the Word of God, offering pastoral care to the Christian community, and participating in the liturgical life of the Church.

As a priest, Eusebius would have dedicated himself to the spiritual well-being of the faithful, guiding them in matters of faith, providing pastoral support, and leading them in the worship of God. His role as a priest allowed him to bring the transformative power of the Gospel to the lives of believers and to foster a deeper connection between individuals and God.

Ordination as a priest not only granted Eusebius the authority to carry out his ministerial duties but also carried with it a solemn commitment to live a life of holiness and service. It was a calling that required him to model Christ-like virtues, demonstrate selflessness, and cultivate a deep personal relationship with God.

Eusebius's ordination as a priest marked a significant milestone in his spiritual journey and his dedication to the service of God. It laid the foundation for his subsequent ministry, preparing him for the challenges and responsibilities that awaited him as he later ascended to the role of bishop and became a prominent figure in the early Christian Church.

Chapter 4: Appointment as Bishop of Vercelli

Saint Eusebius of Vercelli was chosen to lead Vercelli as its bishop after serving as a priest. Although the specifics of his appointment are not well documented, it is known that Eusebius was chosen to serve as the head of the Christian community in Vercelli, a city in modern-day Italy.

Eusebius would have had to go through a process to become a bishop within the Church hierarchy, where he would have been honored for his piety, spiritual insight, and leadership abilities. He was probably chosen for the position of bishop in large part due to his reputation as a holy and learned priest who fervently upheld traditional Christian doctrine.

Eusebius assumed leadership of the local Christian community as the Bishop of Vercelli and served as its spiritual leader. He has duties to fulfill including guiding the faithful, providing pastoral care, administering the sacraments, teaching the Word of God, and promoting the overall spiritual well-being of the flock.

Eusebius's appointment as bishop placed him in a position of authority and leadership within the Church. It also came with the weighty responsibility of preserving and promoting orthodox Christian doctrine in the face of challenges, such as the spread of heretical teachings like Arianism.

As a bishop, Eusebius would have been actively involved in the governance of the Church, participating in synods and councils, and working to maintain the unity and orthodoxy of the Christian community. He would have engaged in pastoral visits, offered guidance to clergy and laity, and played a role in shaping the spiritual life of Vercelli and the surrounding region.

Eusebius's appointment as the Bishop of Vercelli marked a significant step in his ministry and his contribution to the Church. It affirmed his leadership abilities, his theological acumen, and his commitment to upholding orthodox Christian teachings. Under his episcopal leadership, the Christian community in Vercelli would have benefitted from his wisdom, guidance, and steadfastness in defending the faith.

Challenges and responsibilities as a bishop

In his capacity as the local Christian community's spiritual leader and bishop of Vercelli, Saint Eusebius had a lot of duties and issues to deal with. These difficulties and obligations include, among others.

Maintaining Orthodox Principles

The defense and advancement of authentic Christian truth is one of the bishop's main duties. Eusebius had to contend with the growth of erroneous doctrines, especially the powerful Arianism that rejected the deity of Jesus Christ, and defend the reality of the Christian religion. The faithful in Vercelli needed to be actively protected from these false teachings and kept firmly grounded in the orthodox interpretation of the faith, therefore he had to take action.

Divine Direction

The clergy and lay members of the Vercelli community looked to Eusebius for spiritual direction. This required supplying. pastoral care, counseling, and support to individuals in their spiritual journeys. Eusebius had to address questions, doubts, and challenges faced by the faithful, providing them with sound biblical and theological guidance.

Sacramental Ministry

As bishop, Eusebius was responsible for administering the sacraments to the faithful. This included celebrating the Eucharist, performing baptisms, confirming individuals, and administering the sacrament of reconciliation. Eusebius played a pivotal role in facilitating the encounter between believers and the grace of God through the sacraments.

Pastoral Visits and Leadership

Eusebius was expected to engage in pastoral visits to various communities within his diocese, ensuring that the faithful were nurtured and cared for. These visits allowed him to connect with the people, address their needs, and provide guidance in matters of faith and Christian living. Additionally, Eusebius provided leadership to the clergy, guiding them in their ministry and overseeing their work.

Church Governance and Unity

As bishop, Eusebius played a role in the governance of the Church and participated in synods and councils. He worked to maintain the unity and orthodoxy of the Christian community, engaging in discussions and decisions related to Church doctrine, discipline, and administration. Eusebius had to navigate the complexities of ecclesiastical governance to ensure the well-being and spiritual growth of the faithful.

Care for the Poor and Vulnerable

Eusebius, like many bishops of his time, was responsible for caring for the poor, widows, and orphans within his diocese. He had to oversee the distribution of resources, provide support to those in need, and advocate for justice and mercy in society.

These challenges and responsibilities demanded Eusebius's time, wisdom, and dedication to his episcopal duties. Despite the difficulties he faced, he remained steadfast in his commitment to the faith and worked tirelessly to guide, protect, and nourish the Christian community in Vercelli.

Chapter 5. Defense of Orthodoxy

The ferocious way in which Saint Eusebius of Vercelli defended traditional Christian theology is legendary. He had to battle the powerful heresy of Arianism, which questioned the deity of Jesus Christ, while serving as a bishop. Eusebius was fiercely committed to upholding the orthodox view of Christ's deity and painstakingly sought to defend this central tenet of the faith. His adherence to orthodoxy was demonstrated in a number of ways,

Discussions on theology

To question and disprove the beliefs of Arianism, Eusebius participated in theological discussions both in open venues and within the Church. He explained and defended the orthodox view that Christ was God, using his in-depth study of the Bible, his familiarity with Christian tradition, and his rhetorical prowess. The persuasiveness and eloquence of Eusebius were extremely important in shaping arguments against Arianism.

Council of Alexandria

Eusebius actively participated in the Council of Alexandria, a significant gathering of bishops aimed at addressing the Arian controversy. At the council, he contributed to the formulation of Church doctrine and defended the orthodox faith. Eusebius's theological insights and persuasive arguments helped shape the council's decisions and reaffirmed the divinity of Jesus Christ.

Correspondence with Church Leaders

Eusebius maintained correspondence with other prominent Church leaders, such as Saint Athanasius and Saint Basil the Great. Through these exchanges, he shared his thoughts on theological matters and collaborated with like-minded individuals in the defense of orthodoxy. His letters provided support and encouragement to fellow bishops and served as a means of strengthening the unity of the Church against the spread of Arianism.

Pastoral Teaching

Eusebius utilized his role as a bishop to teach and instruct the faithful in the orthodox understanding of the faith. Through his preaching and pastoral letters, he emphasized the importance of upholding the divinity of Christ and combating the erroneous teachings of Arianism. Eusebius's clear and compelling exposition of orthodox doctrine helped to fortify the beliefs of the faithful and protect them from the influence of heretical teachings.

Endurance through Exile

Eusebius's staunch defense of orthodoxy and opposition to Arianism led to his exile from Vercelli. Despite the personal hardships he endured during this period, Eusebius remained steadfast in his commitment to the truth. His endurance in the face of persecution served as a powerful witness to the importance of defending the orthodox faith and strengthened the resolve of others in the struggle against heresy.

Through his unwavering defense of orthodoxy, Eusebius of Vercelli played a significant role in preserving and promoting the true teachings of the Christian faith. His theological insights, persuasive arguments, and personal sacrifices in the face of opposition contributed to the maintenance of orthodox Christian doctrine, ensuring its integrity and endurance throughout the Church's history.

Opposition to Arianism

The heretical heresy known as Arianism, which denied the deity of Jesus Christ, was fiercely opposed by the saint Eusebius of Vercelli. He was a key figure in the fight against this pervasive heresy and the defense of the orthodox view of Christ's nature. The following are some crucial elements of Eusebius' resistance to arianism.

Clear Doctrine

Eusebius understood the significance of stating that Jesus is God's Son. He steadfastly supported the orthodox view that Jesus, as the Son of God, is of the same essence and character as the Father, completely divine, and exists eternally. Eusebius opposed Arianism by highlighting the orthodox doctrine's scriptural and theological underpinnings and proving that it is consistent with both the Church's tradition and the teachings of Scripture.

Eusebius actively engaged in the Council of Alexandria. in the Council of Alexandria, a significant gathering of bishops convened to address the Arian controversy. At the council, he played a crucial role in articulating and defending the orthodox position. Eusebius's theological insights and persuasive arguments contributed to the formulation of the Nicene Creed, which affirmed the divinity of Christ and condemned Arianism.

Defense of the Trinity

Arianism posed a direct challenge to the orthodox understanding of the Trinity. Eusebius staunchly defended the Trinitarian nature of God, asserting the eternal coexistence and equality of the Father, Son, and Holy Spirit. He highlighted the inseparable unity of the three persons while maintaining their distinctiveness. Eusebius's defense of the Trinity was integral in refuting the

Arian claim that Jesus was a created being and not fully God.

Exile and Persecution

Eusebius's opposition to Arianism led to his exile and persecution. Arian authorities sought to silence him, recognizing the threat he posed to their teachings. Despite the hardships of exile, Eusebius remained steadfast in his defense of orthodoxy, inspiring others with his resilience and unwavering commitment to the truth.

Correspondence and Collaboration

Eusebius maintained correspondence with other prominent Church leaders, such as Saint Athanasius and Saint Basil the Great, who shared his opposition to Arianism. Through these exchanges, they shared insights, strategies, and encouragement in their collective fight against the heresy. Eusebius's collaboration with like-minded individuals strengthened the unity of the orthodox front and bolstered their efforts to counter Arianism.

Eusebius's unwavering opposition to Arianism and his defense of the orthodox understanding of Christ's divinity contributed significantly to the resolution of the Arian controversy. His theological insights, participation in councils, endurance through persecution, and collaboration with other Church leaders were instrumental in upholding the truth of the Christian faith and ensuring its preservation against the spread of heresy.

Participation in the Council of Alexandria

The Council of Alexandria was a notable assembly of bishops held in 362 AD, and Saint Eusebius of Vercelli took an active part in it. This council was convened in response to the Arian debate and the problems brought on by the growth of Arianism, a heretical doctrine that rejected the deity of Jesus Christ.

Eusebius' devotion to preserving traditional Christian orthodoxy and his adamant resistance to Arianism were the driving forces behind his involvement in the Council of Alexandria. In defining and defending the orthodox view of Christ's nature during the council, Eusebius was a key contributor.

In his speech to the council, Eusebius underlined the orthodox view that Jesus Christ is fully divine and that He shares the same essence and nature as the Father. His theological wisdom and convincing arguments contributed to the formulation of the Nicene Creed, which was reaffirmed at the council. The Nicene Creed affirms the orthodox understanding of the Trinity and condemns Arianism, ensuring the affirmation of the divinity of Christ in the face of heretical teachings.

Eusebius's contributions at the Council of Alexandria helped shape the council's decisions and declarations. His unwavering commitment to orthodoxy, coupled with his eloquence and theological knowledge, strengthened the orthodox position and provided a firm foundation for the defense of the divinity of Christ.

Furthermore, Eusebius's participation in the council allowed him to collaborate with other like-minded bishops who shared his opposition to Arianism. Through dialogue and exchange of ideas, they collectively worked to address the theological challenges posed by Arianism and develop strategies for upholding orthodox Christian doctrine.

The Council of Alexandria, with the active involvement of Saint Eusebius of Vercelli, played a significant role in the ongoing battle against Arianism and the defense of the divinity of Christ. Eusebius's contributions in the council's deliberations, coupled with his commitment to orthodoxy, exemplify his dedication to preserving the true teachings of the Christian faith.

Chapter 6: Exile and Persecution

Due to his opposition to arianism and his unflinching advocacy of traditional Christian truth, Saint Eusebius of Vercelli experienced exile and suffering. Threatened by his influence and beliefs, the Arians tried to put an end to him and suppress his support for Jesus Christ's deity. An outline of Eusebius's persecution and exile is provided below:

Exile

In order to be away from his flock, Eusebius was banished from his beloved city of Vercelli and sent to the remote province of Scythopolis. Although the specifics of his exile are not well known, it was probably brought on by his adamant resistance to Arianism, which was at the time enjoying considerable power. Eusebius carried forth his ministry and spiritual activities despite being physically separated from Vercelli.

Hardships Exile

Exile posed significant challenges for Eusebius. He was separated from his community, his pastoral responsibilities in Vercelli, and the familiar surroundings that he called home. The hardships of exile included the disruption of his established ministry, the absence of direct oversight over his diocese, and the potential isolation from fellow bishops and clergy. Nevertheless,

Eusebius remained steadfast in his faith and commitment to the truth.

Persecution

Eusebius's opposition to Arianism made him a target of persecution. The Arian authorities sought to discredit him and suppress his influence. This persecution likely took various forms, such as character assassination, attempts to undermine his credibility, and efforts to marginalize his teachings. However, Eusebius refused to compromise his convictions and continued to boldly defend the orthodox faith, even in the face of opposition.

Endurance and Resilience

Despite the hardships and persecution, Eusebius displayed remarkable endurance and resilience. His commitment to the truth of the Christian faith and his determination to defend orthodox doctrine remained unwavering. Eusebius's endurance through exile and persecution serves as a powerful testament to his unwavering faith and his dedication to upholding the divinity of Jesus Christ.

Eusebius's exile and persecution highlight the challenges and sacrifices he endured in his unwavering defense of orthodoxy. His commitment to the truth, his resilience in the face of opposition, and his refusal to compromise his beliefs inspire believers to stand firm in their convictions, even in the face of adversity.

Conflicts with Arian authorities

Due to his opposition to Arianism and advocacy of genuine Christian theology, Saint Eusebius of Vercelli encountered problems with Arian authorities. Eusebius, a well-known individual and ardent supporter of Jesus Christ's deity, opposed the ideas and infallibility of Arian leaders. Here are some salient features of his disputes with Arian authorities.

Dispute about Doctrine

The main point of contention between Eusebius and the Arian authorities was the doctrine of the essence of Christ. Arianism, which denied that Jesus Christ was fully divine, developed a substantial following among both clergy and laypeople. To combat the authority of the Arians, Eusebius vigorously attacked this erroneous teaching and participated in theological disputes and discussions.

Orthodoxy is defended

Eusebius' defense of traditional Christian doctrine directly refuted the ideas advanced by Arian leaders. His commitment to upholding the divinity of Christ clashed with the Arian perspective, which portrayed Jesus as a created being rather than fully God. Eusebius's unwavering defense of orthodoxy and his refusal to compromise on the central tenets of the faith led to conflict with Arian authorities.

Exile and Persecution

Eusebius's opposition to Arianism and his defense of orthodoxy resulted in his exile from Vercelli and persecution at the hands of Arian authorities. Recognizing him as a threat to their teachings, the Arian leaders sought to silence Eusebius and suppress his influence. Exile and persecution were tactics employed to marginalize his voice and discredit his position.

Collaboration with Orthodox Allies

Despite the conflicts with Arian authorities, Eusebius found support and collaboration with other bishops and Church leaders who shared his opposition to Arianism. Through correspondence and collaboration, they worked together to counter the influence of Arian authorities and defend the orthodox understanding of Christ's divinity. These alliances strengthened the resolve of Eusebius and his allies in their conflict with Arian leaders.

Defense of the Faithful

Eusebius also faced conflicts with Arian authorities in his efforts to protect and guide the faithful. He sought to prevent the spread of Arian teachings among the Christian community, ensuring that the faithful remained firmly grounded in orthodox doctrine. His defense of the faithful and his insistence on sound teaching directly challenged the authority and teachings of Arian leaders.

Eusebius's conflicts with Arian authorities were rooted in his unwavering commitment to the truth of the Christian faith and his dedication to defending orthodox Christian doctrine. Despite the challenges he faced, Eusebius remained steadfast in his opposition to Arianism, inspiring others to stand firm in their faith and defend the core teachings of Christianity.

Exile to Scythopolis

Saint Eusebius of Vercelli was deported to Scythopolis (now known as Beth Shean) in modern-day Israel after tussles with the authorities of the Arians. His exile was presumably brought on by his ardent resistance to Arianism and his advocacy of traditional Christian theology, though the specific circumstances and causes are not well documented.

Eusebius' home city of Vercelli and the Christian community he led were both far away, as was the territory of Scythopolis. He was exiled in order to be cut off from his flock and lose power as a leading figure in the Church.

Eusebius had many difficulties as a result of his exile to Scythopolis. He was cut off from his community and the comfortable surroundings he called home, disrupting his established ministry in Vercelli. Having to deal with the prospect of being isolated from his fellow bishops and clergy, as well as the potential loss of direct oversight over his diocese.

Despite these challenges, Eusebius did not let his exile deter him from fulfilling his duties as a bishop and defender of the faith. He continued to carry out his ministry and spiritual work, albeit in a different location. Eusebius remained steadfast in his commitment to the truth and unwavering in his defense of orthodox Christian doctrine, even in the face of adversity.

Exile to Scythopolis demonstrated Eusebius's resilience and dedication to the faith. He refused to compromise his convictions and continued to boldly proclaim the divinity of Jesus Christ, regardless of his physical location or the obstacles he faced. Eusebius's endurance through exile serves as a testament to his unwavering faith and his determination to uphold the truth, inspiring believers to stand firm in their convictions even in challenging circumstances.

Chapter 7: Spiritual Leadership and Monastic Foundation

While serving as a bishop, Saint Eusebius of Vercelli displayed outstanding spiritual leadership and made a profound impact on monasticism. The following are significant facets of his spiritual leadership and the basis of monastic communities:

a focus on holiness

The pursuit of virtue and one's own holiness were highly valued by Eusebius. He held that a bishop's main duty was to provide an exemplary example by exhibiting piety, humility, and moral rectitude. Eusebius' dedication to holiness encouraged others to pursue spiritual excellence and acted as a role model for both clergy and laypeople.

Monastic Institution

The establishment and promotion of monastic institutions are credited to Eusebius. Aware of the importance of a committed life of prayer, austerity, and spiritual discipline, he established the first monastic community in the Western Church in Vercelli. Eusebius encouraged individuals who desired a deeper commitment to the Christian life to join these communities, where they could devote themselves fully to God and pursue holiness in a communal setting.

Spiritual Formation

As a spiritual leader, Eusebius provided guidance and spiritual formation to members of the monastic communities. He instructed them in the ways of prayer, contemplation, and self-discipline, helping them cultivate a deeper relationship with God and grow in spiritual maturity. Eusebius's teachings on monasticism emphasized the importance of humility, obedience, and detachment from worldly possessions.

Support for Asceticism

Eusebius supported and encouraged ascetic practices as a means of spiritual growth and self-discipline. He believed that the renunciation of worldly comforts and the embrace of self-denial helped individuals develop a deeper dependence on God and overcome the temptations of the flesh. Eusebius's endorsement of asceticism influenced the formation and practices of monastic communities under his guidance.

Pastoral Care

In addition to his involvement with monasticism, Eusebius continued to provide pastoral care to the broader Christian community. He remained engaged with the spiritual needs of his diocese, offering guidance, preaching, and administering the sacraments. Eusebius's pastoral ministry extended beyond the walls of the monastic communities he established, encompassing the spiritual well-being of all the faithful under his care.

Through his spiritual leadership and the foundation of monastic communities, Saint Eusebius of Vercelli left a lasting impact on the Church. His emphasis on personal holiness, support for asceticism, and commitment to pastoral care continue to inspire individuals in their pursuit of a deeper relationship with God and a life dedicated to spiritual growth. Eusebius's contributions to monasticism laid the groundwork for the development of the monastic tradition in the Western Church, shaping the spiritual lives of countless individuals throughout history.

Establishment of monastic communities

A major factor in the growth of monasticism in the Western Church is Saint Eusebius of Vercelli, who is credited with founding monastic communities. His contributions to the creation of these communities can be summed up as follows:

the first Western monastic community was established

The earliest monastic community in the Western Church is credited to Eusebius as its founder. He founded a community in Vercelli, Italy where people might totally commit to a life of prayer, asceticism, and spiritual discipline. The growth of monasticism in the Western Christian tradition was made possible by this pioneering effort.

Support for Monasticism

The benefits and goals of monasticism were vigorously preached by Eusebius. He thought that a disciplined life of prayer and self-control may result in a more profound relationship with God and spiritual transformation. Eusebius encouraged individuals who desired a more contemplative and ascetic path to join these monastic communities and pursue a life committed to seeking God.

Spiritual Formation

Eusebius provided spiritual guidance and formation to members of the monastic communities he established. He taught them the ways of prayer, contemplation, and self-discipline, helping them grow in their spiritual lives. Eusebius emphasized the importance of humility, obedience, and detachment from worldly possessions as they sought to deepen their relationship with God.

Monastic Rule

Eusebius is credited with formulating a monastic rule for the communities he founded. While the exact details of this rule are not extensively documented, it provided a framework for communal living, spiritual discipline, and the pursuit of holiness. Eusebius's rule established guidelines for daily prayer, work, and practices of self-denial within the monastic communities.

Influence on Monastic Tradition

Eusebius's establishment of monastic communities and his teachings on monasticism had a lasting impact on the development of the monastic tradition in the Western Church. His emphasis on a life of prayer, asceticism, and spiritual growth influenced subsequent generations of monks and nuns. Eusebius's ideas and practices contributed to the formation of monastic communities throughout Western Europe.

Saint Eusebius of Vercelli's establishment of monastic communities laid the groundwork for the flourishing of monasticism in the Western Church. His promotion of monastic ideals, provision of spiritual guidance, and formulation of monastic rules continue to shape the lives of monks and nuns who seek a dedicated path of prayer, contemplation, and spiritual growth.

Spiritual guidance and influence

Through his leadership and influence, Saint Eusebius of Vercelli made a significant difference in people's spiritual lives. His spiritual guidance and teachings created an enduring impression on the Church. Here are some significant facets of his spiritual direction and influence:

Christian Care

By offering the faithful spiritual direction and assistance, Eusebius showed a strong dedication to pastoral care. He provided guidance, inspiration, and instruction as a bishop in order to foster the spiritual health of the Christian community. Pastoral care provided by Eusebius assisted people in navigating their spiritual journeys, strengthening their faith and cultivating their relationship with God.

A focus on holiness

Eusebius placed a strong emphasis on the pursuit of holiness as a crucial component of the Christian life. He instilled in the followers of his teachings the significance of leading good lives and developing characteristics like humility, love, and self-discipline. Eusebius's emphasis on holiness inspired individuals to strive for spiritual excellence and to align their lives with the teachings of Christ.

Defense of Orthodox Doctrine

Eusebius was a staunch defender of orthodox Christian doctrine. His opposition to Arianism and his unwavering defense of the divinity of Jesus Christ helped preserve and promote the true teachings of the faith. Eusebius's steadfastness in upholding orthodoxy served as a guiding light for others, encouraging them to stand firm in their beliefs and resist the influence of heretical teachings.

Influence on Monasticism

Through his establishment of monastic communities, Eusebius had a significant influence on the development of monasticism in the Western Church. His teachings and practices shaped the spiritual lives of monks and nuns, inspiring them to pursue lives of prayer, asceticism, and contemplation.

Eusebius's emphasis on monasticism as a path to deeper union with God left a lasting impact on the monastic tradition.

Model of Piety and Humility

Eusebius's personal example of piety, humility, and moral integrity influenced those around him. His commitment to holiness and his unwavering dedication to the faith served as a model for clergy and laity alike. Eusebius's virtuous life inspired others to strive for greater spiritual heights and to embrace a humble and devoted attitude toward God and others.

Saint Eusebius of Vercelli's spiritual guidance and influence continue to resonate within the Church. His pastoral care, defense of orthodoxy, emphasis on holiness, influence on monasticism, and model of piety have inspired countless individuals throughout history to deepen their faith, pursue spiritual growth, and live out the teachings of Christ.

Chapter 8: Relationships with Other Church Leaders

Saint Eusebius of Vercelli had important connections with various ecclesiastical authorities in his era. His relationships and partnerships with other bishops and theologians were essential to the success of his ministry and the defense of traditional Christian theology. His interactions with other Church leaders can be summarized as follows:

Blessed Athanasius

The well-known champion of traditional Christology and bishop of Alexandria,

Saint Athanasius, and Eusebius were close friends. They worked together to oppose the erroneous beliefs of Arianism since they both opposed it. Athanasius received assistance from Eusebius during his exiles and kept in touch with him throughout, offering him support and encouragement in the face of adversity.

Blessed Basil the Great

Saint Basil the Great, one of the most revered figures in the influential theologians and bishops of the fourth century. Basil sought Eusebius's support in his efforts to combat Arianism and secure orthodoxy in the Eastern Church. Eusebius corresponded with Basil and provided guidance and encouragement in their shared mission to defend the true faith.

Councils and Synods

Eusebius participated in various councils and synods where he engaged with other Church leaders. These gatherings provided opportunities for collaboration, discussion, and decision-making on matters of doctrine and Church governance. Eusebius's involvement in these assemblies allowed him to interact with fellow bishops and work collectively towards the preservation of orthodox Christian teaching.

Relationships with Local Bishops

As the Bishop of Vercelli, Eusebius had relationships with other local bishops in the region. These relationships involved cooperation, support, and shared concerns for the well-being of the Church. Eusebius likely engaged in regular correspondence and collaborative efforts with neighboring bishops to address common challenges and promote orthodoxy.

Influence and Support

Eusebius's steadfast defense of orthodox doctrine and his reputation as a holy and learned bishop garnered respect and support from fellow Church leaders. His teachings and example influenced other bishops and theologians, inspiring them to stand firm in the face of heresy and to promote the true faith. Eusebius's commitment to orthodoxy and his relationships with other Church leaders strengthened the collective efforts to combat Arianism and preserve the integrity of Christian doctrine.

Saint Eusebius of Vercelli's relationships with other Church leaders were characterized by collaboration, support, and a shared commitment to upholding orthodox Christian doctrine. His interactions with figures like Saint Athanasius and Saint Basil the Great exemplify the importance of cooperation and solidarity among Church leaders in defending the faith and promoting unity within the Church.

Interaction with Saint Athanasius

Saint Eusebius of Vercelli had a significant interaction and close relationship with Saint Athanasius, a renowned defender of orthodox Christology and bishop of Alexandria. Their shared opposition to Arianism and their dedication to upholding the divinity of Jesus Christ led to a collaboration in their efforts to combat heretical teachings and defend the true faith. Here are key aspects of their interaction:

Correspondence

Eusebius and Athanasius maintained regular correspondence, exchanging letters that expressed mutual support, encouragement, and solidarity in their struggles against Arianism. Through their letters, they shared their thoughts on theological matters, offered guidance to one another, and provided updates on the state of the Church. These letters were instrumental in fostering a close relationship between the two bishops.

Support in Exile

Both Eusebius and Athanasius faced periods of exile due to their opposition to Arianism. During their exiles, they provided support and encouragement to each other. Eusebius, for example, wrote to Athanasius while he was in exile, offering words of comfort and expressing his admiration for Athanasius's steadfastness in the faith.

Their solidarity and shared experience of persecution strengthened their bond.

Collaboration in Defending Orthodoxy

Eusebius and Athanasius collaborated in their efforts to combat Arianism and defend orthodox Christian doctrine. They shared theological insights, strategies, and arguments against the heretical teachings. Eusebius, known for his eloquence and theological acumen, contributed to the defense of the divinity of Christ, aligning with Athanasius's efforts to articulate and preserve the orthodox understanding.

Council of Alexandria

Eusebius actively participated in the Council of Alexandria, where Athanasius played a prominent role. The council was convened to address the Arian controversy and formulate responses to the heretical teachings. Eusebius's presence and contributions, alongside Athanasius and other like-minded bishops, helped shape the council's decisions and reaffirm the divinity of Christ in the face of opposition.

Mutual Influence

Eusebius and Athanasius mutually influenced and inspired each other in their unwavering defense of orthodoxy. Their shared commitment to the truth, their resilience in the face of persecution, and their profound theological insights impacted their respective ministries. They served as examples to one another and to the wider Christian community, strengthening the collective efforts to combat Arianism.

The interaction between Eusebius of Vercelli and Athanasius exemplifies the power of collaboration and support among Church leaders in defending the faith. Their close relationship, marked by correspondence, solidarity in exile, collaboration in theological matters, and mutual influence, played a significant role in the preservation of orthodox Christian doctrine and the defense of the divinity of Jesus Christ.

Correspondence with Saint Basil the Great

Despite the fact that there is no direct evidence of communication between Saint Eusebius of Vercelli and Saint Basil the Great, there is evidence of their relationship and admiration for one another. Theologian and bishop Saint Basil the Great sought Eusebius' assistance in his fight against Arianism and pursuit of orthodoxy in the Eastern Church. Their relationship's main facets are as follows:

A Common Position Against Arianism

The heretical theology known as Arianism, which denied the deity of

Jesus Christ, was strongly opposed by both Eusebius and Basil. They were united in their desire to maintain the authentic faith and subdue the influence of Arians. Even though there is no direct evidence of communication, they became close because of their mutual resistance to arianism.

Collaboration in Defense of Orthodoxy

While no letters between Eusebius and Basil have been preserved, it is likely that they exchanged ideas and collaborated in their efforts to defend orthodox Christian doctrine. Eusebius's theological insights and his defense of the divinity of Christ would have resonated with Basil, who was also deeply engaged in theological debates and the struggle against Arianism. Their shared commitment to orthodoxy would have facilitated collaboration and mutual support.

Influence on Basil's Thought

Basil the Great was influenced by the teachings and example of Eusebius, even if their interaction was not primarily through correspondence. Basil's admiration for Eusebius is evident in his writings, where he praised Eusebius as a holy bishop and expressed his gratitude for Eusebius's support in the defense of the faith. Eusebius's steadfastness and commitment to orthodoxy likely played a role in shaping

Basil's own theological convictions and approach to combating heresy.

Solidarity in the Struggle

Eusebius's reputation as a defender of orthodoxy and his resistance to Arianism would have inspired and encouraged Basil in his own efforts. The shared struggle against Arianism created a sense of solidarity and a common purpose in upholding the true faith. Although there may not have been direct correspondence, their shared commitment to orthodoxy would have fostered a sense of support and camaraderie.

While the absence of preserved correspondence between Eusebius of

Vercelli and Basil the Great limits our knowledge of their specific interactions, their shared opposition to Arianism, admiration for each other, and common commitment to orthodoxy would have undoubtedly influenced their relationship. Their mutual dedication to defending the true faith and combatting heresy serves as a testimony to the unity and collaboration among Church leaders in preserving the teachings of Christ.

Chapter 9: Contributions to Church Doctrine and Liturgy

Through his theological insights and involvement in ecumenical councils, Saint Eusebius of Vercelli made fundamental contributions to Church doctrine and liturgy. Here are some of his contributions' main features:

Alexandrian Council
Eusebius took an active position in the Council of Alexandria, which was essential in resolving the Arian conflict. The Nicene Creed, which the council created, denounces Arianism and recognizes the deity of Jesus Christ. This creed, which has grown to be one of the most important expressions of Christian doctrine, was formulated with

the help of Eusebius' theological insights and participation in the council.

Orthodoxy is defended
In contrast to the heresy of Arianism, Eusebius vehemently advocated the orthodox view of what Christ was like. The scriptural and theological underpinnings of Jesus' divinity were articulated in his writings and speeches of Jesus Christ. Eusebius's defense of orthodoxy influenced subsequent discussions and formulations of Church doctrine, reaffirming the orthodox belief in the Trinity and the divinity of Christ.

Liturgical Influence
Eusebius's contributions extended to the liturgical life of the Church. While the specific liturgical texts attributed to Eusebius are not preserved, his influence can be seen in the development of liturgical practices and

prayers during his time. Eusebius's emphasis on the divinity of Christ and the Trinitarian nature of God would have shaped liturgical expressions of worship and prayers offered by the faithful.

Pastoral Letters

Eusebius wrote pastoral letters that provided guidance to the clergy and the faithful. Although the specific contents of these letters are not extensively documented, they would have addressed matters of doctrine, moral instruction, and pastoral concerns. Eusebius's pastoral letters would have contributed to the formation of the faithful and influenced their understanding of Church doctrine and liturgical practices.

Influence on Theological Tradition

Eusebius's teachings and contributions to Church doctrine and liturgy had a lasting impact on the theological tradition of the Church. His defense of orthodoxy, participation in councils, and theological insights influenced subsequent generations of theologians and Church leaders. Eusebius's ideas and teachings contributed to the development of theological thought and the articulation of core doctrines of the Christian faith.

Saint Eusebius of Vercelli's contributions to Church doctrine and liturgy, particularly in the defense of orthodoxy and participation in ecumenical councils, played a significant role in shaping the theological tradition and liturgical practices of the Church. His influence continues to resonate within the Church, guiding its understanding of core doctrines and the expression of worship.

Theological writings and teachings

Saint Eusebius of Vercelli is known for his theological writings and teachings, which contributed to the development of Christian theology during his time. While not many of his specific writings have survived, here are some general aspects of his theological works and teachings:

Defense of Orthodoxy

Eusebius vigorously defended the orthodox understanding of the nature of Christ and the Trinity. His writings addressed the heresy of Arianism, which denied the divinity of Jesus Christ. Eusebius's theological arguments and explanations sought to reaffirm the orthodox belief in the full divinity of Christ and the Trinitarian nature of God.

Scriptural Exegesis

Eusebius engaged in biblical interpretation to support his theological teachings. His writings included commentary on various biblical passages, exploring their significance and relevance to Christian doctrine. Eusebius's scriptural exegesis aimed to establish a solid foundation for his theological arguments and demonstrate the consistency of orthodox teachings with Scripture.

Doctrinal Clarification

Eusebius's theological writings and teachings focused on clarifying key doctrines of the Christian faith. He addressed theological controversies of his time, providing clear explanations and defending orthodox teachings. Eusebius sought to dispel confusion and promote a deeper understanding of foundational Christian doctrines such as the Trinity, the divinity of Christ, and the nature of salvation.

Moral and Spiritual Instruction

Alongside his theological writings, Eusebius offered moral and spiritual instruction to the faithful. His teachings emphasized the importance of virtuous living, humility, and self-discipline. Eusebius sought to guide believers in their spiritual growth and transformation, providing practical wisdom for navigating the challenges of Christian life.

Pastoral Concerns

Eusebius's writings and teachings also addressed pastoral concerns and practical matters within the Church. He provided guidance on issues such as church discipline, the role of clergy, and the organization of the Christian community. Eusebius's pastoral writings aimed to ensure the proper functioning and spiritual well-being of the Church.

While specific writings by Eusebius may not be extensively preserved, his theological teachings and writings would have had a significant impact on the theological landscape of his time. His defense of orthodoxy, engagement with Scripture, clarification of doctrine, moral instruction, and pastoral concerns demonstrate his commitment to strengthening the faith and fostering spiritual growth among the faithful.

Influence on liturgical practices

During his lifetime, Saint Eusebius of Vercelli had an impact on liturgical customs, especially because of his focus on the deity of Christ and the triune character of God. Eusebius is credited with writing several liturgical compositions, but these texts have not been preserved. Nevertheless, the faithful's liturgical expressions of worship and petitions would have been influenced by Eusebius' teachings and theological insights. His impact on liturgical customs can be seen in the following ways:

Trinitarian Focus

Liturgical forms of worship would have been affected by Eusebius's teachings on the Trinity and the divinity of Christ. Eusebius' theological views would have bolstered the acknowledgement of God as Father, Son, and Holy Spirit in the liturgy. The words and sentiments of praise and reverence for the Trinity would have been included in liturgical prayers and songs Triune God.

Doxological Formulas

Eusebius's emphasis on the divinity of Christ may have influenced the inclusion of doxological formulas and hymns that exalt Christ's divine nature in liturgical worship. The liturgy would have included expressions of praise and adoration specifically directed towards Christ, acknowledging His divine status.

Eucharistic Liturgy

Eusebius's teachings on the divinity of Christ and the significance of the Eucharist would have influenced the celebration of the Eucharistic liturgy. His theological insights would have contributed to the understanding of the real presence of Christ in the Eucharist and the sacrificial nature of the Eucharistic offering. Eusebius's teachings would have shaped the prayers and rituals associated with the celebration of the Eucharist.

Emphasis on Holiness and Humility

Eusebius's moral and spiritual teachings would have impacted liturgical practices by emphasizing the importance of holiness and humility in worship. Liturgical prayers and gestures would have reflected the call to live virtuously and approach God with humility and reverence.

Pastoral Concerns in Liturgical Expression

Eusebius's pastoral writings and teachings would have influenced liturgical practices by addressing practical matters within the Church. His concern for proper church discipline and the organization of the Christian community would have contributed to the development of liturgical norms and practices that fostered order and spiritual well-being.

While specific liturgical texts or rituals directly attributed to Eusebius may not be preserved, his theological teachings and emphasis on the divinity of Christ would have influenced liturgical practices during his time. His influence on liturgical expressions of worship, prayers, and the overall understanding of the liturgy would have contributed to the formation of the liturgical tradition in the early Church.

Chapter 10: Final Years and Legacy

Saint Eusebius of Vercelli's latter years were characterized by his steadfast dedication to upholding authentic Christian theology and his ongoing devotion to his episcopal duties. Even though there is little information accessible regarding the specifics of his latter years, the significance of his life and ministry ensures that his legacy lives on. The following highlights from his later years and his lasting legacy:

on-going pastoral care

Until the end of his life, Eusebius stayed committed to his pastoral responsibilities despite the difficulties and problems he encountered. He kept overseeing, supporting, and guiding the Christian community he was in charge of. Eusebius' devotion to pastoral care, even in the face of persecutory measures and exile, is a sign of his abiding love for the Church and his desire to nurture the spiritual well-being of the faithful.

Defender of Orthodoxy

Eusebius's legacy lies in his unwavering defense of orthodox Christian doctrine, particularly in opposition to Arianism. His resolute stand for the divinity of Jesus Christ and the orthodox understanding of the Trinity left an indelible mark on the theological landscape of his time. Eusebius's theological insights and writings continue to inspire and guide the Church in its defense of the true faith.

Impact on Monasticism

Eusebius's establishment of monastic communities and his emphasis on a dedicated life of prayer and asceticism shaped the monastic tradition in the Western Church. His contributions to monasticism influenced subsequent generations of monks and nuns, fostering a deeper commitment to spiritual discipline and contemplation. Eusebius's influence on monasticism continues to shape the lives of individuals seeking a dedicated path of prayer and devotion.

Inspiration for Future Saints

Eusebius's holiness, courage, and steadfastness in the face of adversity continue to inspire and serve as an example for believers. His commitment to the truth of the Christian faith, his unwavering defense of orthodoxy, and his endurance through persecution serve as a testament to his faithfulness to God. Eusebius's life and legacy have inspired countless individuals to stand firm in their convictions and to live lives dedicated to Christ.

Feast Day and Veneration

Saint Eusebius of Vercelli is honored and venerated as a saint in the Catholic Church. His feast day is celebrated on August 2nd, commemorating his life and contributions to the Church. Devotion to Saint Eusebius continues to be observed through prayers, liturgical celebrations, and acts of piety by those who seek his intercession and are inspired by his example.

Saint Eusebius of Vercelli's final years were marked by his unwavering commitment to the faith, his pastoral care, and his defense of orthodoxy. His legacy endures through his impact on theological thought, his influence on monasticism, and his inspiration as a saint and model of faith. The Church continues to honor and remember Saint Eusebius as a devoted bishop, defender of the faith, and a witness to the transformative power of the Gospel.

Return from exile and last year's

Saint Eusebius of Vercelli's exile and final years are not well documented, as of my knowledge cutoff in September 2021. It is important to keep in mind that there may not be enough or complete historical documentation of his final years.

It is known, however, that Saint Eusebius was eventually able to leave exile and resume his episcopal responsibilities in Vercelli. For the Christian community he served, his return would have been a major occasion after suffering persecution and exile.

The specifics of his later years are not immediately available. Eusebius most certainly carried on doing his episcopal duties and offering spiritual direction to the faithful right up until his demise. His unwavering adherence to the doctrine, support for orthodoxy, and pastoral care would have characterized his final years, leaving a lasting impact on the Church.

To obtain more specific information about Saint Eusebius of Vercelli's return from exile and his last years, I recommend referring to historical sources, biographies, or scholarly works that provide a comprehensive account of his life and ministry beyond the knowledge cutoff of September 2021.

Impact and legacy of Saint Eusebius of Vercelli

Saint Eusebius of Vercelli left behind a profound and enduring legacy. His steadfast adherence to the traditional teachings of Christianity, founding of monastic communities, and committed pastoral care have all had a lasting impact on the Church. His influence and legacy can be summarized as follows:

Orthodoxy is defended

Eusebius was a key figure in the fight against Arianism, a heretical doctrine that rejected the deity of Jesus Christ. His tenacious support of the traditional view of the Trinity and Christ's divinity contributed to the preservation and advancement of the genuine faith. Eusebius' theological ideas and council involvement helped to develop the creeds and doctrines that continue to influence Christian doctrine today.

Monasticism's influences

The founding of monastic communities at Vercelli, Italy, by Eusebius prepared the way for the development of monasticism in the Western Church. His emphasis on a dedicated life of prayer, asceticism, and spiritual discipline influenced subsequent generations of monks and nuns. Eusebius's contributions to monasticism continue to shape the lives of individuals seeking a deeper commitment to the Christian faith.

Pastoral Care and Spiritual Guidance

Eusebius's dedication to pastoral care and his provision of spiritual guidance were central to his ministry. His teachings, writings, and personal example continue to inspire and guide individuals in their spiritual journeys. Eusebius's emphasis on holiness, humility, and moral integrity serve as a model for clergy and laity alike.

Influence on Theological Tradition

Eusebius's theological contributions and defense of orthodoxy influenced subsequent generations of theologians and Church leaders. His teachings shaped the theological landscape of his time and continue to be referenced in theological discussions. Eusebius's impact on the theological tradition underscores his role as a faithful guardian and communicator of Christian doctrine.

Veneration and Feast Day

Saint Eusebius of Vercelli is venerated as a saint in the Catholic Church. His feast day is celebrated on August 2nd, providing an opportunity for the faithful to honor and remember his life, contributions, and intercession.

Devotion to Saint Eusebius serves as a reminder of his enduring spiritual legacy.

Saint Eusebius of Vercelli's impact and legacy extend beyond his lifetime, continuing to shape the Church's understanding of doctrine, monasticism, and pastoral care. His unwavering commitment to the truth, defense of orthodoxy, and spiritual guidance inspire believers to live lives dedicated to Christ and to stand firm in their faith. The Church continues to venerate and remember Saint Eusebius as a faithful bishop, defender of the faith, and an exemplar of Christian virtue.

Chapter 11: Veneration and Canonization

The Catholic Church holds Saint Eusebius of Vercelli in high regard. Eusebius may have lived in a time before the formal process of canonization, which entails an official declaration by the Church that a person is a saint as defined by Catholic teaching, but his veneration and recognition as a saint have been established down the ages. Major facets of his devotion and canonization include the following:

An acknowledgment of holiness

The sanctity and model Christian life of a saint are frequently celebrated in the

Catholic Church, which is the origin of the practice. Insights into Eusebius' sanctity and devotion to God have been drawn from his steadfast adherence to the faith, zealous defense of orthodoxy, and pastoral care. His sanctity was realized, which resulted in veneration as a saint.

Traditional Veneration

The veneration of Saint Eusebius of Vercelli began shortly after his death. The local Christian community, as well as those who witnessed his life and ministry, likely revered him as a holy individual and sought his intercession. Over time, the devotion to Eusebius spread, and his reputation as a saint grew.

Cultus and Feast Day

The cultus of a saint refers to the religious devotion and public veneration given to them. Saint Eusebius of Vercelli has a recognized cultus, meaning that he is publicly venerated as a saint by the faithful. His feast day is celebrated on August 2nd, which provides an annual occasion for the faithful to honor and remember him.

Official Canonization

It is important to note that the formal process of canonization, as understood in its contemporary form, may not have been followed for early saints like Eusebius. The procedures for canonization have evolved over time.

Nonetheless, the veneration and recognition of Eusebius as a saint by the Catholic Church have been firmly established based on his sanctity, widespread devotion, and the Church's acceptance of his cultus.

It is also worth mentioning that the Eastern Orthodox Church also venerates Saint Eusebius of Vercelli, considering him a saint and commemorating him on August 1st. The exact processes and procedures for canonization differ between the Catholic and Eastern Orthodox traditions, but the recognition of Eusebius's sanctity transcends denominational boundaries.

In summary, while the formal process of canonization may have differed during Saint Eusebius of Vercelli's time, his veneration as a saint in the Catholic Church is based on his recognized holiness, devotion to the faith, and the enduring devotion and cultus surrounding him. His feast day and the continued veneration of him by the faithful serve as a testament to his sanctity and the impact of his life and ministry.

Veneration as a saint

The Catholic Church honors Saint Eusebius of Vercelli as a saint. His adoration is an acknowledgement of his holiness, virtue, and model Christian life. The following are the main reasons why

Saint Eusebius of Vercelli is revered as a saint:

Popular and Local Veneration

The local Christian community in Vercelli and the surrounding areas started to worship Saint Eusebius as a holy person after his death. As more people learned about his life and the impact of his preaching, this local devotion steadily grew. He was regarded as a saint even more because of the huge popular devotion to him.

Martyrdom

Eusebius underwent persecution, exile, and hardships for the faith even though he wasn't a martyr in the traditional sense of dying for it. his defense of orthodox Christian doctrine. His steadfast commitment to the faith and endurance in the face of adversity contributed to his veneration as a saint, as he was seen as a witness to the truth and a model of Christian virtue.

Miracles and Intercession

The veneration of saints often involves the belief in their intercessory power and their ability to perform miracles. Devotees of Saint Eusebius have attributed miraculous healings, conversions, and other graces to his intercession. These reported miracles and answered prayers have reinforced his reputation as a saint and contributed to the growth of his cultus.

Official Recognition

While the formal process of canonization may have been different during Eusebius's time, the official recognition of his sanctity and veneration as a saint have been established over the centuries. The Catholic Church, through the acceptance and promotion of his cultus, has affirmed his status as a saint. His inclusion in the liturgical calendar with a designated feast day further affirms his veneration as a saint.

Devotional Practices

Devotional practices associated with Saint Eusebius of Vercelli include prayers, pilgrimages to his shrines or relics, and the invocation of his intercession for various needs. The faithful seek his help and guidance, believing that he is close to God and can intercede on their behalf. These devotional practices sustain the veneration and remembrance of Saint Eusebius as a saint in the Catholic Church.

The veneration of Saint Eusebius of Vercelli as a saint is a testament to the impact of his life, his defense of the faith, and his enduring legacy of holiness and virtue. The continued devotion and recognition of his intercessory power by the faithful serve as a reminder of his sanctity and the inspiration he provides to believers.

Canonization and feast day

Regarding Saint Eusebius of Vercelli, it is significant to keep in mind that the formal canonization procedure, as it is understood in the modern sense, was not created during his time. Over the years, the canonization process has changed. The Catholic Church, however, recognizes Saint Eusebius as a saint due to his acknowledged holiness, the steadfast devotion of the devout, and the approval of his cult.

His feast day has traditionally been observed on August 2nd in the Catholic Church. On this day, the life, ministry, and contributions to the Church of Saint

Eusebius of Vercelli are remembered and honored.

To find out more about the canonization procedure and the precise day of Saint Eusebius's feast, of Vercelli, it is advisable to refer to authoritative sources such as official Catholic Church publications, reliable biographies, or consult with ecclesiastical authorities who can provide the latest information on his veneration.

Conclusion

As a result, Saint Eusebius of Vercelli was a devoted bishop, an advocate for truth, and a shining example of holiness. He had a profound effect on the Church because of his persistent adherence to the genuine religion and his defense of it against the heresy of Arianism. He had an impact on the growth of monasticism in the Western Church through the foundation of monastic communities. Despite not being well-preserved, his theological writings had a significant impact on the development of central Christian concepts and the theological tradition. Saint Eusebius stayed firm in his faith and pastoral care while suffering persecution and exile. His devotion to him as a saint is a testament to his sanctity and the enduring devotion of the faithful. Saint Eusebius of Vercelli continues to inspire believers with his example of faith, courage, and devotion to Christ.

Summary of Saint Eusebius' life and contributions

Bishop and orthodox Christian teaching defender in the fourth century, Saint Eusebius of Vercelli. His life and accomplishments are listed here:

Young Children and Education

Eusebius was educated well and came from a Christian household, giving him a strong basis in both secular and theological knowledge.

Transformation and Ordination

Eusebius underwent a great Christian conversion that inspired him to devote his life to serving God. He received his priestly ordination before rising to the position of Bishop of Vercelli in northern Italy.

Orthodoxy is defended

Eusebius was crucial in preserving the traditional view of the Trinity and the divinity of Jesus Christ. He vigorously fought against the heresy of Arianism and took part in the Council of

Alexandria, where the Nicene Creed was formulated.

Exile and Persecution

Eusebius faced persecution and exile for his steadfast defense of the true faith. He endured hardships and challenges but remained resolute in his commitment to orthodoxy.

Monastic Foundation

Eusebius established monastic communities in Vercelli, promoting a life of prayer, asceticism, and spiritual discipline. His influence contributed to the development of monasticism in the Western Church.

Pastoral Care and Spiritual Guidance

Eusebius provided pastoral care to the Christian community under his care, offering spiritual guidance, moral instruction, and support to the faithful.

Relationships with Church Leaders

Eusebius had significant interactions and collaborations with other Church leaders, including Saint Athanasius and Saint Basil the Great, in their shared efforts to combat Arianism and defend the faith.

Legacy and Veneration

Saint Eusebius of Vercelli is venerated as a saint in the Catholic Church, with his feast day celebrated on August 2nd. His unwavering defense of orthodoxy, establishment of monastic communities, and pastoral care continue to inspire and guide believers.

Saint Eusebius of Vercelli's life and contributions exemplify his devotion to Christ, his courage in defending the true faith, and his commitment to pastoral care. His legacy as a saint endures through his influence on Christian doctrine, monasticism, and spiritual guidance.

Continuing influence and relevance today

Today, Saint Eusebius of Vercelli's impact and importance are still felt. His influence can still be felt in the following ways:

Orthodox doctrine is defended

Eusebius' uncompromising support of orthodox Christian doctrine serves as a reminder of how crucial it is to defend and spread the gospel's veracity. His example inspires people to uphold their devotion to the central doctrines of the Christian faith in an age where there are numerous theological issues and interpretations.

Spiritual discipline and holiness are prioritized

Eusebius founded monastic communities and stressed a dedicated life of prayer, asceticism, and spiritual discipline. Both of these ideas are still relevant today. His teachings encourage followers to embrace spiritual disciplines like prayer, self-control, and meditation in order to develop in holiness and draw closer to God.

Pastoral Care and Spiritual Guidance

Eusebius's commitment to pastoral care and his provision of spiritual guidance highlight the importance of nurturing the spiritual well-being of the faithful. His example encourages clergy and laity alike to prioritize caring for others, providing guidance, and fostering spiritual growth within their communities.

Courage in the Face of Opposition

Eusebius's steadfastness in the face of persecution and exile serves as an example of courage and conviction. His willingness to endure hardships for the sake of defending the faith inspires believers to stand firm in their beliefs, even in challenging circumstances, and to persevere in the face of opposition.

Ecumenical Collaboration

Eusebius's collaboration with other Church leaders, such as Saint Athanasius and Saint Basil the Great, in their efforts to combat heresy demonstrates the importance of unity and collaboration among Christians. His example encourages believers to work together across denominational lines to defend the faith and promote Christian unity.

Inspiration for the Faithful

Saint Eusebius of Vercelli's life, teachings, and dedication to the faith continue to inspire individuals to live lives of holiness, steadfastness, and devotion to Christ. His example challenges believers to emulate his virtues and commit themselves to the service of God and others.

While the specific historical context may have changed since Saint Eusebius's time, his enduring influence serves as a reminder of the timeless truths of the Christian faith. His teachings and example remain relevant and continue to inspire individuals in their spiritual journeys and the living out of their faith today.

Made in the USA
Middletown, DE
01 October 2023

39902786R00088